DANIEL BOONE

As a boy of nine, Daniel Boone could not stay away from the forest. Farming was not the life he wanted. Daniel Boone wanted to be a hunter. It became difficult for the Boone family to find food and they started across the country to find a new place to live. Daniel became a good hunter. Soon he heard about a new land called Kentucky. Daniel Boone knew he would find it. In the next years he made trips over mountains and met with many dangers. His story is an exciting adventure you will enjoy reading.

Other SEE AND READ
Beginning to Read Biographies:

ABRAHAM LINCOLN

GEORGE WASHINGTON

POCAHONTAS

CHRISTOPHER COLUMBUS

JOHN FITZGERALD KENNEDY

NATHAN HALE

A SEE AND READ

Beginning to Read Biography

DANIEL BOONE

by Patricia Miles Martin

illustrated by Glen Dines

G. P. Putnam's Sons   New York

For David and Dick Lind

Text © 1965 by Patricia Miles Martin
Illustrations © 1965 by Glen Dines
Library of Congress Catalog Card Number: 65-10873
MANUFACTURED IN THE UNITED STATES OF AMERICA
Published simultaneously in the Dominion of Canada
by Longmans Canada Limited, Toronto
07209

DANIEL BOONE

A nine-year-old boy leaned against a tree and thought about running away.

He looked at the cows that fed in a meadow near a forest. Not far away, his mother worked in their cornfield.

She called to him.

"Don't forget to look after those cows, Daniel," she said.

At last, she went into the cabin.

He waited a minute, then away he ran.

He ran as fast as a wildcat into the forest. He ran fast, for he knew if she saw him, she would call him back.

In the forest, Daniel Boone lay on the ground and did not move.

"I'll be as still as a stone," he said to himself. "Maybe I'll see a bear or an Indian."

Daniel was as brown as the ground.
He lay so still that the squirrels and
rabbits didn't see him. A deer went
by, almost near enough to touch.

For a long time, he didn't move.
Then he heard the moo of a cow and
hurried back to the meadow.

He counted the cows and found they were all there.

He looked to see if his mother knew he had been away. She stood by the cabin door.

"Daniel," she said, "you should not go into the forest without asking."

"I know," he said. "I can't stay away. It is as if the forest calls and I have to go."

She shook her head. "You will never be a farmer like your father and your brothers."

That night, Daniel helped milk the cows. He didn't like working on a farm. He knew he didn't want to be a farmer. He liked only the forest.

He thought about this.

The Pennsylvania forest was full of
good things. There was wood for fire
and animals for food.

"I will be a hunter," he said.

He knew about other things to be found in the forest. There were the slow, sleepy snakes. There were Indians. Daniel had seen Indians painted for war.

After supper that night, he thought
how it would be to sleep in the forest.
The hard ground would be his bed
and the sky, his roof. He would need
a rifle to keep at his side.

This was what he wanted most. He
wanted to be in the forest with a rifle
of his own.

When Daniel was twelve years old,
his father gave him a rifle.

Daniel went into the forest every day. He knew where wild animals went for food and water. He knew where to find bear and deer.

The forest was his teacher, and Daniel grew wise in the way of the forest.

At home, he tried to learn to read and write. He was able to read, but he could never learn to spell.

"Leave the spelling to the girls," his father said. "Daniel will take care of the hunting."

And Daniel took care of the hunting.

As time went on, it became hard to find enough wild game for food. The family left Pennsylvania and started across country to find a new place to live.

For two years they rode looking for the land they wanted.

They found a place to live on the
Upper Yadkin River in North Caro-
lina. Here were so many wild animals,
that Daniel found hunting too easy to
be fun.

He could kill twenty deer in one
morning.

Other settlers came and made their homes where Indians had long lived. The Indians were angry about this.

From over the mountains, they followed a secret path and came, painted for war. They lay in hiding in the wilderness, ready to fight.

Other people were ready to fight, too.

The French knew of this wild country. They came from the north to claim it for their own.

From the Atlantic Coast, the American colonists sent young George Washington to fight them.

The settlers hurried to help him, and Daniel Boone was with them.

The settlers and George Washington's men were on one side. The French and the Indians were on the other.

After a short, hard fight, the settlers were pushed back and Daniel Boone went home.

More and more settlers came to the
Upper Yadkin River. With them was
Rebecca, a girl who became the wife
of Daniel Boone.

It was at this time that Daniel Boone heard about another land. It was called Kentucky.

It was a hunting ground of the Indians. It was said that one might find it in the west, through the Cumberland Gap.

Daniel knew that someday he would find this place, for the wilderness always called him.

His friends wanted him to go. "Find this place called Kentucky," they said, "and we will follow you."

In the next ten years, Rebecca and Daniel had many children. And all this time Daniel was busy hunting, to feed his family.

So these many years were to pass before Daniel Boone started for Kentucky. He wanted land which he could take for his own. At last the day came when he started.

He left Rebecca and his children at home. Five men went with him.

He led them up and over the mountains. They found the secret Indian path that led to the Cumberland Gap.

At the top of the mountain, Daniel looked down and saw a beautiful land. Beside the river, the canes grew higher than a man's head, and buffaloes fed there. The path that these animals made through the canebrake was as wide as a street.

Here was land for the taking.

This was Kentucky.

Daniel thought that he would soon
cut a road through this wilderness.
Then he could bring his family, and
his friends would follow.

From summer to winter, the men saw no Indians. One cold day, Daniel and his friend John Stuart went into the canebrake. They went to find buffaloes.

As they walked along a buffalo path, they heard the sound of horses. They came face to face with Indians.

Daniel Boone said to John, "Don't show that you are afraid. Act brave and you *are* brave."

With tomahawks in their hands, the Indians made Boone take them to his camp.

On the way, he talked to the Indians in a loud voice. The men who were still in camp heard him and knew that Indians were coming. As Daniel wanted his friends to do, they ran away.

The Indians took the food and horses they found there.

"Go home, brother," an Indian said. "Go home and stay. This is Indian land."

Daniel and John walked until night came. Then Daniel stopped and looked back.

"Let's go find that Indian camp and get our horses," he said.

In the still of night, they went back to find the camp. They took their own horses and rode away.

In the morning, they stopped to let
their horses rest. The Indians came
galloping through the forest and
caught them again.

One night, they all sat around the campfire.

Boone looked at the sleepy Indians, then at the canebrake by the river.

"It's hard to find a man in the canebrake," he said.

He and John ran for the canebrake and hid there. The Indians followed and hunted for them a long time, but they found no one.

After the Indians left, Daniel and John went on their way.

It was not long before they found their own men. They made a new camp not far from the old Indian path.

One day, John Stuart went hunting for food.

He did not come back.

When Daniel Boone went for him, he found only cold ashes of a campfire.

One by one Boone's men left for home.

For a time, Daniel hunted alone. Now he knew almost as much about Kentucky as the Indians knew. And he knew about the Indians. They did not want others to live on this land.

They would kill for land they claimed
for their own hunting.

Daniel Boone went back to his home
and to his family.

One day, he started for Kentucky again. This time, he took his wife and children with him. Many of their friends went along.

With enough settlers going to Kentucky, it could be made a safe place to live.

They all followed the old Indian path to the Cumberland Gap. Men with their rifles were first. The girls and their mothers followed behind them. Boys and dogs went last to watch the cows and pigs.

They were on their way when Indians killed James, first of the Boone children.

In Kentucky, they started building
a stockade where they might be safe
from the Indians.

Again and again, the Indians came.
Arrows of fire fell over the wall.

Boys ran to fight the fire, while the sound of rifles rang through the stockade.

Then the Indians would leave, as quickly as they had come.

Boone knew they would come again and again.

One summer Daniel Boone and his
men started to make a new road. The
Wilderness Road, it was called. They
cut through mile after mile of forest.

They made the road wide enough for a wagon to pass over. Now, more and more settlers could follow to Kentucky.

One winter's day, when Daniel
Boone was hunting, the Indians
caught him again.

Again, he did not show that he was
afraid.

He laughed when he saw them.

They thought he was happy to see them, and took him to their camp. They gave him an Indian name.

"You are now an Indian," they said. "You are Big Turtle."

They set a little Indian sister to watch over him. Little Sister would tell them if he tried to get away.

Where Boone went, there went Little Sister.

He was with the Indians a long time, for Little Sister was always there. From morning to night, she followed him.

"There is no one who sees as much as a child can see," he said.

A day came when the Indian men went hunting and left Boone in camp. He walked over to his horse.

"My boy," a woman called. "What are you doing? Where are you going?"

"I am going home to my own family," he said.

As he galloped away, he could hear Little Sister's loud cry.

At home, his friends were surprised to see him. So much time had gone by, they thought he had been killed by the Indians.

More settlers came to Kentucky —
too many for Daniel Boone.

He turned to face the West. He had
heard of a wild land where he would
find buffalo again. He would find bear
and deer. He and Rebecca went on.

They lived in a new cabin in the new land. Their dishes were made of wood, their forks of the canebrake.

There were bear and buffalo in this land.

Here the Indians came.

Again, Daniel Boone did not show
that he was afraid. He laughed to see
them and his laughing worked magic.

Friendly, the Indians went on their
way.

When Daniel Boone was very old,
the forest still called him.

He had what he wanted.

This was the way he liked to live.

He was in the wilderness, looking
for bear, with his rifle across his knees.

KEY WORDS

arrows

buffalo

cabin

canebrake

canoe

claim (claimed)

colonists

farmer

hunter (hunting)

meadow

rifle

settlers

snakes

stockade

tomahawks

wilderness

The Author

PATRICIA MILES MARTIN describes herself as a "compulsive writer." Her first poem was accepted by a Missouri newspaper when she was seven. In 1957 she began writing for children. More than a dozen of her books have been published, including SEE AND READ BIOGRAPHIES of *John Fitzgerald Kennedy, Abraham Lincoln* and *Pocahontas*. Mrs. Martin and her husband live in San Mateo, California.

The Artist

GLEN DINES has twelve juvenile books to his credit, including historical nonfiction such as *Overland Stage, Indian Pony* and *Bull Wagon*. Mr. Dines lives with his wife and two children in San Rafael, California.